Mom-O ❀ Morfar ♡ Mormor ☀ Muddy ♡ Mzee ☾ Nama ☆ Na...

Nanny ☀ Nanuzzo ☾ Ni Ni ☆ Noni ❀ Nonna ♡ Nonno ☀

Opa ❀ Paeter ♡ Papa ☀ Papaw ☾ Pépé ☆ Pop ❀ Popa...

Pop-pop ☾ Poppy ☆ Pua-pua ❀ Saba ♡ Saftah ☀ Teta ☾ Umpa ☆ Ya-Ya ❀ Zaide

Abuela ☀ Abuelito ☾ Abuelo ☆ Baba ❀ Babapapa ♡ Babbo ☀ Bammy ☾ Beanpa

Bema ☆ Bibie ❀ Boppa ♡ Boppy ☀ Bubbie ☾ Buchi ☆ Budgy ❀ Bumpy ♡ Bungy

Counbu ☀ Counya ☾ Da ☆ Damama ❀ Far Far ♡ Far Mor ☀ Ga ☾ G'dad ☆ Gamma

Gammon ❀ Gammpa ♡ Gammy ☀ Gan-Gan ☾ GG ☆ Gia ❀ Gigi ♡ Gone-gone ☀ GP

Gram ☾ Gramma ☆ Grammy ❀ Grampy ♡ Grand Pa D ☀ Granda ☾ Granddaddy

Grandmère ☆ Grandpère ❀ Grandy ♡ Granny-Pie ☀ Granpa Bud ☾ Groovy Granny

Guma ☆ Helcha ❀ Jiddo ♡ Maeter ☀ Mama Manny ☆ Mamaw ❀ Mami

Mamita ♡ Mamo ☀ Medzmama ☾ MeMe ☆ Mémé ❀ Meter ♡ Mimi ☀ Mimsi

Miss Melle ☾ Moetje ☆ Mom-mom ❀ Mom-O ♡ Morfar ☀ Mormor ☾ Muddy

Mzee ☆ Nama ❀ Nana ♡ Nana Banana ☀ Nanny ☾ Nanuzzo ☆ Ni Ni ❀ Noni

Nonna ♡ Nonno ☀ Nucci ☾ Oma ☆ Omah ❀ Opa ♡ Paeter ☀ Papa ☾ Papaw

Pépé ☆ Pop ❀ Popalita ♡ Popose ☀ Poppa ☾ Pop-pop ☆ Poppy ❀ Pua-pua ♡ Saba

Saftah ☀ Teta ☾ Umpa ☆ Ya-Ya ❀ Zaide ♡ Abuela ☀ Abuelito ☾ Abuelo ☆ Baba

Babapapa ❀ Babbo ♡ Bammy ☀ Beanpa ☾ Bema ☆ Bibie ❀ Boppa ♡ Boppy

Bubbie ☀ Buchi ☾ Budgy ☆ Bumpy ❀ Bungy ♡ Counbu ☀ Counya ☾ Da

Damama ☆ Far Far ❀ Far Mor ♡ Ga ☀ G'dad ☾ Gamma ☆ Gammon ❀ Gammpa

Gammy ❀ Gan-Gan ♡ GG ☀ Gia ☾ Gigi ☆ Gone-gone ❀ GP ♡ Gram ☾ Gramma

Abuela ☀ Abuelito ☾ Abuelo ☆ Baba ❀ Babapapa ♡ Babbo ☀ Bammy ☾ Bear Bema ☆ Bibie ❀ Boppa ♡ Boppy ☀ Bubbie ☾ Buchi ☆ Budgy ❀ Bumpy ♡ Bur Counbu ☀ Counya ☾ Da ☆ Damama ❀ Far Far ♡ Far Mor ☀ Ga ☾ G'dad ☆ Gam Gammon ❀ Gammpa ♡ Gammy ☀ Gan-Gan ☾ GG ☆ Gia ❀ Gigi ♡ Gone-gone ☀ Gram ☾ Gramma ☆ Grammy ❀ Grampy ♡ Grand Pa D ☀ Granda ☾ Granddad Grandmère ☆ Grandpère ❀ Grandy ♡ Granny-Pie ☀ Granpa Bud ☾ Groovy Gran Guma ☆ Helcha ❀ Jiddo ♡ Maeter ☀ Mama Manny ☆ Mamaw ❀ Mami ♡ Mam Mamo ☀ Medzmama ☾ MeMe ☆ Mémé ❀ Meter ♡ Mimi ☀ Min Miss Melle ☾ Moetje ☆ Mom-mom ❀ Mom-O ♡ Morfar ☀ Mormor ☾ Mud Mzee ☆ Nama ❀ Nana ♡ Nana Banana ☀ Nanny ☾ Nanuzzo ☆ Ni Ni ❀ N Nonna ♡ Nonno ☀ Nucci ☾ Oma ☆ Omah ❀ Opa ♡ Paeter ☀ Papa ☾ Pap Pépé ☆ Pop ❀ Popalita ♡ Popose ☀ Poppa ☾ Pop-pop ☆ Poppy ❀ Pua-pua ♡ So Saftah ☀ Teta ☾ Umpa ☆ Ya-Ya ❀ Zaide ♡ Abuela ☀ Abuelito ☾ Abuelo ☆ Bo Babapapa ❀ Babbo ♡ Bammy ☀ Beanpa ☾ Bema ☆ Bibie ❀ Boppa ♡ Bop Bubbie ☀ Buchi ☾ Budgy ☆ Bumpy ❀ Bungy ♡ Counbu ☀ Counya ☾ Damama ☆ Far Far ❀ Far Mor ♡ Ga ☀ G'dad ☾ Gamma ☆ Gammon ❀ Gamm Gammy ❀ Gan-Gan ♡ GG ☀ Gia ☾ Gigi ☆ Gone-gone ❀ GP ♡ Gram ☾ Gram Grammy ☀ Grampy ☾ Grand Pa D ☆ Granda ❀ Granddaddy ♡ Grandmère ☀ Grandp Grandy ☾ Granny-Pie ☆ Granpa Bud ❀ Groovy Granny ♡ Guma ☀ Helcha ☾ Ji Maeter ☆ Mama Manny ♡ Mamaw ☀ Mami ☾ Mamita ☆ Mamo ❀ Medzma MeMe ♡ Mémé ☀ Meter ☾ Mimi ☆ Mimsi ☆ Miss Melle ♡ Moetje ☀ Mom-

Grandparents

ARE THE GREATEST BECAUSE...

BY

ADELE
ARON
GREENSPUN

&

JOANIE
SCHWARZ

DUTTON
CHILDREN'S
BOOKS
—
NEW YORK

To my children and stepchildren, who blessed me with grandchildren
To my editor, Meredith, who answered my dream
And always, to Bert
A.A.G.

To Don, Lee, and Dean—
the most important men in my life
J.S.

Library of Congress Cataloging-in-Publication Data
Greenspun, Adele Aron.
Grandparents are the greatest because—/ Adele Aron Greenspun and Joanie Schwarz.
p. cm.
Summary: Photographs illustrate and text describes some of the interactions and activities
of grandchildren with their grandparents.
ISBN 0-525-47131-6
[1. Grandparents—Fiction.] I. Schwarz, Joanie. II. Title.
PZ7.G85195Gr2003 [E]—dc21 2002041592

Published in the United States 2003 by Dutton Children's Books,
a division of Penguin Young Readers Group
345 Hudson Street, New York, New York 10014
www.penguin.com

Designed by Irene Vandervoort

Manufactured in China
First Edition

10 9 8 7 6 5 4 3 2

AUTHOR'S NOTE

When I learned I was going to be a grandmother, I would smile at my reflection in store windows, trying on my new name as I walked by. *Grandmother…*

The day I held my first grandchild's warm body, gift-wrapped in blankets, and touched her tiny fingers, I knew I was in love for the rest of my life. As each new baby was born, the thrill multiplied. My grandchildren became the only subjects I wanted to photograph. The faces of Ariel, Lee, Frances, and Dean brightly fill the places at the holiday table of those who are no longer here. My new status in life became the wellspring for this book.

Grandparents begin to love you before you are even born. Your relationship is special; different from mothers and fathers, sisters and brothers, aunts and uncles, cousins and friends.

If you ever wonder from whom you inherited your blue eyes, tall body, skill with a ball or a musical instrument, grandparents are the ones who hold these answers. They are keepers of family history and can tell tales about your parents when they were children, or about relatives who died before you were born. History comes alive when grandparents share stories of how they lived when they were your age. You can be teachers for each other. Grandparents give you a past to remember, and you give them a future to envision—a gift only youth and age can give to each other.

ACKNOWLEDGMENTS

The list is long, and my debt is great to the grandparents and grandchildren who graciously granted interviews and permitted me to photograph them. My appreciation to the members of the Greater Philadelphia Wordshop Studio for their encouragement and support. I thank the following schools for allowing me access to students who provided insights and metaphors:

MERION ELEMENTARY SCHOOL, MERION, PA
SIDWELL FRIENDS SCHOOL, WASHINGTON, D.C.
COOPERTOWN SCHOOL, HAVERTOWN, PA
EXTON SCHOOL, EXTON, PA
THE PINELLAS COUNTY DAY SCHOOL, ST. PETERSBURG, FL
B'NAI ISRAEL SCHOOL, CLEARWATER, FL
THE HILLEL SCHOOL, TAMPA, FL

"Grandparents are like candy—you always need more." —Laura

they let you stay up past midnight

"My grandchildren are just yummy." —Zelda G.

and eat ice cream for breakfast.

"When my grandson was adopted, I was so excited.

I knew the pleasure it was going to be." —Morrie R.

They don't mind getting splashed

"I want to have fun with my grandson—play in the ocean and roll in the sand." —Shelby T.

or buried in cold sand.

"Being with Grandpa is like a comedy show." —Jonathan

they give you the giggles

"I drop everything when the grandchildren are here.

Nothing else is important." —Diane A.

and let you make a bunch of noise.

"Sophie is like medicine—she takes the pain away." —Shelley S.

They cheer you up with smooches

"When I'm with Mimi,

I feel like I've been declared president." —Jason

and big, warm squeezes.

They keep you from falling,

"Grandparents are the only ones who can give unconditional love." —Roberta K.

and when you do, they help you up.

"Being with Bammy is an adventure." —Margaret

elephants don't scare them,

"It's wonderful to have grandchildren because that is how we go on in the world." —Mary K.

and neither do dinosaurs with big, sharp teeth.

"I don't think of Saba as old, because he does stuff like ride bikes and Rollerblade." —Emily

They love to learn new things—

"You could invite me to the opera, but I wouldn't go.

I'd rather go to my granddaughter's talent show." —Gloria Z.

especially if *you* are the teacher.

"I like when Grammy takes me to water aerobics and I quit after five minutes and she keeps going and going." —Adam

They make you feel like the only kid in the world,

"Being with Pepsi-Pop is like being at a big party." —Danielle

even if your family is big.

"I know Uppi is proud of me. He makes me feel like me." —Ian

they tell everyone that you caught the biggest fish

"Granddaddy makes me feel like I'm a special sheep among a flock." —Merissa

and scored the best goal.

"Being with my Dupy is like being with a genie." —Zachary

They can turn pillows into pirate ships

"Oji Chan teaches me Japanese. I teach him English." —Mia

and read your favorite book over and over.

"Being with Gramps is like being alive in the thirties.

He tells neat stories about his youth." —Sammy

They tell amazing stories about the past

"My grandfather was in two wars. He got the Purple Heart and a lot of medals." —Michael

and let you try on their memories.

"When I'm a grandma, I will treat my grandchildren with love—

that's how my Bubbie treats me." —Jenni

grandmas say "Yes," not "Maybe."

"Pop-pop indulges me more than my parents ever would." —David

Grandpas say "Sure!" not "We'll see."

"I teach my grandchildren to respect all cultures." —Barry D.

From Grandpa's shoulders you can see forever.

"Mom-mom is a soft pillow on a hard day." —Frances

In Grandma's arms you feel special and safe.

"I wanted to be called Nana because that's what I called

my grandmother—the connection before and after me." —Magda L.

Grandparents are the greatest because

"Being with Gigi is like seeing spring flowers

after a really long winter." —Jasmine

they're never too busy to listen…

"I could travel anywhere in the world in search of excitement, but there's nothing more exciting than being

with my granddaughters. When they come here, that's excitement to me." —Ben L.

and they never run out of love.

Mom-O ❀ Morfar ♡ Mormor ☀ Muddy ♡ Mzee ☾ Nama ☆ Nana ❀ Nana Banana

Nanny ☀ Nanuzzo ☾ Ni Ni ☆ Noni ❀ Nonna ♡ Nonno ☀ Nucci ☾ Oma ☆ Omah

Opa ❀ Paeter ♡ Papa ☀ Papaw ☾ Pépé ☆ Pop ❀ Popalita ♡ Popose ☀ Poppa

Pop-pop ☾ Poppy ☆ Pua-pua ❀ Saba ♡ Saftah ☀ Teta ☾ Umpa ☆ Ya-Ya ❀ Zaide

Abuela ☀ Abuelito ☾ Abuelo ☆ Baba ❀ Babapapa ♡ Babbo ☀ Bammy ☾ Beanpa

Bema ☆ Bibie ❀ Boppa ♡ Boppy ☀ Bubbie ☾ Buchi ☆ Budgy ❀ Bumpy ♡ Bungy

Counbu ☀ Counya ☾ Da ☆ Damama ❀ Far Far ♡ Far Mor ☀ Ga ☾ G'dad ☆ Gamma

Gammon ❀ Gammpa ♡ Gammy ☀ Gan-Gan ☾ GG ☆ Gia ❀ Gigi ♡ Gone-gone ☀ GP

Gram ☾ Gramma ☆ Grammy ❀ Grampy ♡ Grand Pa D ☀ Granda ☾ Granddaddy

Grandmère ☆ Grandpère ❀ Grandy ♡ Granny-Pie ☀ Granpa Bud ☾ Groovy Granny

Guma ☆ Helcha ❀ Jiddo ♡ Maeter ☀ Mama Manny ☆ Mamaw ❀ Mami

Mamita ♡ Mamo ☀ Medzmama ☾ MeMe ☆ Mémé ❀ Meter ♡ Mimi ☀ Mimsi

Miss Melle ☾ Moetje ☆ Mom-mom ❀ Mom-O ♡ Morfar ☀ Mormor ☾ Muddy

Mzee ☆ Nama ❀ Nana ♡ Nana Banana ☀ Nanny ☾ Nanuzzo ☆ Ni Ni ❀ Noni

Nonna ♡ Nonno ☀ Nucci ☾ Oma ☆ Omah ❀ Opa ♡ Paeter ☀ Papa ☾ Papaw

Pépé ☆ Pop ❀ Popalita ♡ Popose ☀ Poppa ☾ Pop-pop ☆ Poppy ❀ Pua-pua ♡ Saba

Saftah ☀ Teta ☾ Umpa ☆ Ya-Ya ❀ Zaide ♡ Abuela ☀ Abuelito ☾ Abuelo ☆ Baba

Babapapa ❀ Babbo ♡ Bammy ☀ Beanpa ☾ Bema ☆ Bibie ❀ Boppa ♡ Boppy

Bubbie ☀ Buchi ☾ Budgy ☆ Bumpy ❀ Bungy ♡ Counbu ☀ Counya ☾ Da

Damama ☆ Far Far ❀ Far Mor ♡ Ga ☀ G'dad ☾ Gamma ☆ Gammon ❀ Gammpa

Gammy ❀ Gan-Gan ♡ GG ☀ Gia ☾ Gigi ☆ Gone-gone ❀ GP ♡ Gram ☾ Gramma

Abuela ☀ Abuelito ☽ Abuelo ☆ Baba ✿ Babapapa ♡ Babbo ☀ Bammy ☽ Bean
Bema ☆ Bibie ✿ Boppa ♡ Boppy ☀ Bubbie ☽ Buchi ☆ Budgy ✿ Bumpy ♡ Bun
Counbu ☀ Counya ☽ Da ☆ Damama ✿ Far Far ♡ Far Mor ☀ Ga ☽ G'dad ☆ Gam
Gammon ✿ Gammpa ♡ Gammy ☀ Gan-Gan ☽ GG ☆ Gia ✿ Gigi ♡ Gone-gone ☀ G
Gram ☽ Gramma ☆ Grammy ✿ Grampy ♡ Grand Pa D ☀ Granda ☽ Granddad
Grandmère ☆ Grandpère ✿ Grandy ♡ Granny-Pie ☀ Granpa Bud ☽ Groovy Gran
Guma ☆ Helcha ✿ Jiddo ♡ Maeter ☀ Mama Manny ☆ Mamaw ✿ Mami ♡ Mam
Mamo ☀ Medzmama ☽ MeMe ☆ Mémé ✿ Meter ♡ Mimi ☀ Min
Miss Melle ☽ Moetje ☆ Mom-mom ✿ Mom-O ♡ Morfar ☀ Mormor ☽ Mud
Mzee ☆ Nama ✿ Nana ♡ Nana Banana ☀ Nanny ☽ Nanuzzo ☆ Ni Ni ✿ N
Nonna ♡ Nonno ☀ Nucci ☽ Oma ☆ Omah ✿ Opa ♡ Paeter ☀ Papa ☽ Pap
Pépé ☆ Pop ✿ Popalita ♡ Popose ☀ Poppa ☽ Pop-pop ☆ Poppy ✿ Pua-pua ♡ So
Saftah ☀ Teta ☽ Umpa ☆ Ya-Ya ✿ Zaide ♡ Abuela ☀ Abuelito ☽ Abuelo ☆ Ba
Babapapa ✿ Babbo ♡ Bammy ☀ Beanpa ☽ Bema ☆ Bibie ✿ Boppa ♡ Bof
Bubbie ☀ Buchi ☽ Budgy ☆ Bumpy ✿ Bungy ♡ Counbu ☀ Counya ☽
Damama ☆ Far Far ✿ Far Mor ♡ Ga ☀ G'dad ☽ Gamma ☆ Gammon ✿ Gamm
Gammy ✿ Gan-Gan ♡ GG ☀ Gia ☽ Gigi ☆ Gone-gone ✿ GP ♡ Gram ☽ Gram
Grammy ☀ Grampy ☽ Grand Pa D ☆ Granda ✿ Granddaddy ♡ Grandmère ☀ Grandp
Grandy ☽ Granny-Pie ☆ Granpa Bud ✿ Groovy Granny ♡ Guma ☀ Helcha ☽ Jid
Maeter ☆ Mama Manny ♡ Mamaw ☀ Mami ☽ Mamita ☆ Mamo ✿ Medzma
MeMe ♡ Mémé ☀ Meter ☽ Mimi ☆ Mimsi ✿ Miss Melle ♡ Moetje ☀ Mom-m